AF264271

I dedicate all my adventures to all my new Earthling friends!

Zorp you lots!

www.MarshieTheMartian.com

Marshie the Martian floated down into a dusty arena. He heard cheering, stomping, and loud "YEE-HAWS!" "What is this wild Earth party?" he asked. A cowboy smiled. "Welcome to the rodeo, little fella!"

Marshie looked at the cowboy and said,
"I want to be in the rodeo."
The cowboy laughed. "Little fella, only
real cowboys can be in the rodeo!"
Marshie nodded. "I can be a real
cowboy."

POOF!
Marshie tossed Mars dust - POOF! "Now I'm a real cowboy" he shouted. The crowd cheered for the tiny green cowboy.

A huge bull snorted in the chute. Marshie climbed on and whispered, "Hello, giant muscle-moo rocket."

The gate opened. The bull bucked wildly, but Marshie bounced like a rubber ball.

Instead of holding on with one hand, Marshie put both hands in the air. "Look no hands!" he yelled.

The crowd roared with laughter. Even the bull looked confused as Marshie jumped off as the buzzer sounded.

Marshie saw a horse and asked,
"Is this your speedy dirt-runner?"

The rider nodded. Marshie tossed Mars dust - POOF! Now he sat on a tiny floating saddle.

The whistle blew. Marshie zoomed around the barrels - but not on the ground. He floated above them, spinning like a green tornado. "That's not how barrel racing works!" someone shouted. "It does now!" Marshie replied. The crowd cheered wildly for their new favorite cowboy.

Marshie saw clowns in colorful outfits. He tossed Mars dust - POOF! Now he wore giant shoes, a rainbow wig, and a squeaky nose.

"I am Silly Marshie The RODEO CLOWN!"

A bull charged toward him.
Marshie popped his bubble
shield - POOF! The bull bounced
off like a beach ball.

Marshie giggled.
"Bubble power saves the day!"

Marshie juggled baby chickens.

He wore big clown glasses. He honked his nose so loudly the bull stopped charging. The crowd laughed until their sides hurt.

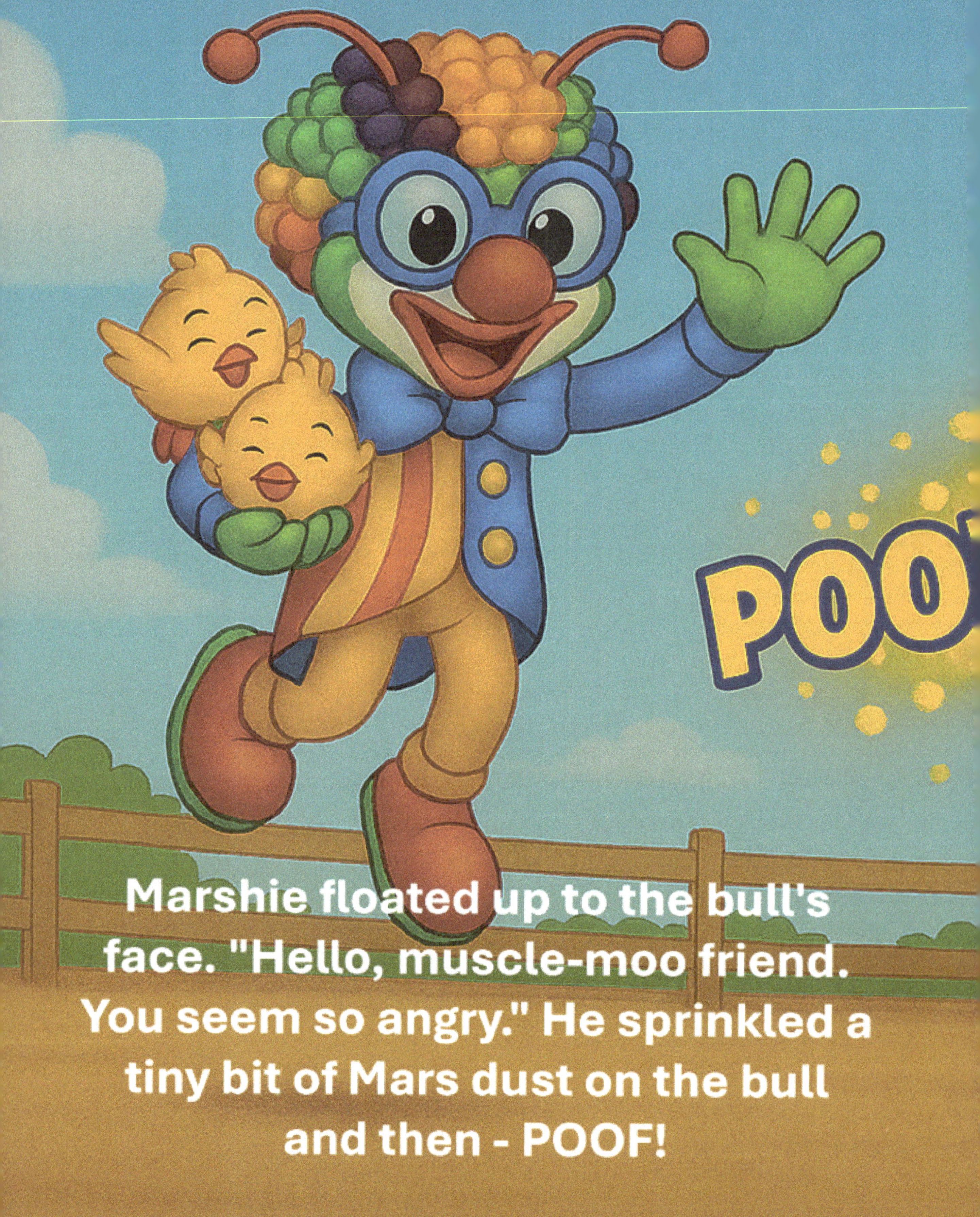

Marshie floated up to the bull's face. "Hello, muscle-moo friend. You seem so angry." He sprinkled a tiny bit of Mars dust on the bull and then - POOF!

POOF!

The bull relaxed and sat down
like a giant puppy.

The bull rolled over and Marshie immediately started to tickle the muscle-moo rocket.

The bull laughed hysterically and the crowd cheered "Bravo-Bravo" for their new favorite cowboy.

Marshie turned back into
his Marshie self.

He zoomed into the air - spinning, flipping, and glowing. He made shapes with Mars dust. Kids pointed and shouted, "Do it again!"

Marshie threw a huge handful of Mars dust - POOF! A giant glowing lasso appeared in the sky. It looped and twirled above the arena like magic. The crowd gasped in amazement.

The cowboys tipped their hats. "Thanks for the show little partner," they said.

Marshie bowed. "You Earth cowboys are brave and very dusty."

Marshie floated into the sky, waving. "I love the rodeo. I'm a real cowboy!"

BYE-BYE
SILLY MARSHIE!

1. What do you call a bull that's taking a nap? **A bulldozer.**

2. Why did the cow bring a pencil to the rodeo? In case it needed to **draw a crowd.**

3. What do you call a horse that lives next door? **A neigh-bor.**

4. Why did the cowboy get in trouble at school? He wouldn't stop horsing around.

5. What do you call a cow that can play the guitar? **A moo-sician.**